THE DOG WRITES
ON THE WINDOW

THE DOG WRITES ON THE WINDOW WITH HIS NOSE and other poems

collected by David Kherdian

pictures by Nonny Hogrogian

Library of Congress Cataloging in Publication Data
Main entry under title:
The Dog writes on the window with his nose and other poems.

    SUMMARY: Twenty-two brief poems by a variety of
American poets.

    1. Children's poetry, American.   [1. American
poetry—Collections]   I. Kherdian, David.
II. Hogrogian, Nonny.   PZ8.3.D675   811'.5'08   76–26516
ISBN 0-590-07448-2

Published by Four Winds Press
A Division of Scholastic Magazines, Inc., New York, N.Y.
Copyright © 1977 by David Kherdian and Nonny H. Kherdian
All rights reserved
Printed in the United States of America
Library of Congress Catalog Card Number: 76–26516
1 2 3 4 5   81 80 79 78 77

For reprint permission, grateful acknowledgment is made to:

Cape Goliard Press for "The Resemblance" by Anselm Hollo from *Maya.*

City Lights Books for "In the Mexican Zoo" by Gregory Corso from
        Gasoline, copyright © 1958 by Gregory Corso; "make it new"
        by Lawrence Ferlinghetti from *Back Roads to Far Towns after
        Basho,* copyright © 1970 by Lawrence Ferlinghetti; "Elephants
        munching" and "The moon had" by Jack Kerouac from
        Scattered Poems, copyright © 1971 by The Estate of
        Jack Kerouac.

Delacorte Press/Seymour Lawrence for "The Pumpkin Tide" and
        "Xerox Candy Bar" by Richard Brautigan from *The Pill versus
        the Springhill Mine Disaster,* copyright © 1968 by Richard
        Brautigan.

Jim Gibbons for "Poem for Cat Haters."

The Giligia Press for "While I write these" by Ray Drew from *Goat Songs,* © 1970 by Ray Drew.

Grey Fox Press for "Redwood Haiku" by Lew Welch from *Ring of Bone,* copyright © 1973 by Donald Allen, Literary Executor of the Estate of Lew Welch.

Harper & Row, Publishers, Inc. for "Note" by William Stafford from *Allegiances,* copyright © 1964 by William Stafford.

Nonny Hogrogian and David Kherdian for "The New Concord Barnyard Poem."

David Kherdian for "Cat" and "Just Now."

Ruth Krauss for "Poem."

Beatrice Roethke Lushington for "Once Upon a Tree" by Theodore Roethke from "Where Knock Is Open Wide" from *Dirty Dinky and Other Creatures,* © 1973 by Beatrice and Stephen Lushington.

Moore Publishing Co., Durham, N.C., for "An Historic Moment" and "On Wearing Ears" from *Nine Black Poets.*

New Directions Publishing Corporation for "Of our visitors—I do not know" by Charles Reznikoff from *By the Waters of Manhattan,* copyright 1934 by Charles Reznikoff and "Poem" by William Carlos Williams from *Collected Earlier Poems,* copyright 1938 by New Directions Publishing Corporation.

Aram Saroyan for "crickets" from *Works,* © 1966 by Aram Saroyan (Lines Press).

Philip Whalen for "Early Spring" from *On Bear's Head,* copyright © 1960, 1965, 1969 by Philip Whalen (Harcourt Brace Jovanovich, Inc. and Coyote/New York).

Contents

POEM

As the cat
climbed over
the top of

the jamcloset
first the right
forefoot

carefully
then the hind
stepped down

into the pit of
the empty
flowerpot

William Carlos Williams

The moon had
a cat's mustache
For a second

Jack Kerouac

Of our visitors—I do not know

which I dislike most:
the silent beetles or these
noisy flies.

Charles Reznikoff

REDWOOD HAIKU

Orange, the brilliant slug—
Nibbling at the leaves of
Trillium

Lew Welch

Elephants munching
   on grass—loving
Heads side by side.

Jack Kerouac

While I write these
Fat little birds
type upon the snow.

Ray Drew

THE NEW CONCORD BARNYARD POEM

three fat geese
bump past the startled deer
thump, thump,
thump, thump, thump...
they're wanted elsewhere!

Nonny Hogrogian and David Kherdian

THE PUMPKIN TIDE

I saw thousands of pumpkins last night
come floating in on the tide,
bumping up against the rocks and
rolling up on the beaches;
it must be Halloween in the sea.

Richard Brautigan

POEM FOR CAT HATERS

catscat

Jim Gibbons

CAT

Missak on his
rocktop moss
covered throne
(in our fern &
flower garden)
sits & catches
flies and keeps
his belly warm

David Kherdian

EARLY SPRING

The dog writes on the window
with his nose

Philip Whalen

POEM

on paper
I write it
on rain

I write it
on stones
on my boots

on trees
I write it
on the air

on the city
how pretty
I write my name

Ruth Krauss

Bumblegoober
Bumblegoober
Bumblegoober
Bumble
BUMBLE
BUMBLEGOOBER Bum
Bumblegoober Bumblegoober Be
Bumblegoober
Bumblegoober

THE RESEMBLANCE

hey did you just see the man

who looked like a camel

we saw in the zoo who looked

just like a man

we saw in the street who

looked at you

just like a camel?

Anselm Hollo

In the Mexican Zoo
     they have ordinary
American cows.

Gregory Corso

XEROX CANDY BAR

Ah,
you're just a copy
of all the candy bars
I've ever eaten.

Richard Brautigan

NOTE

straw, feathers, dust—
little things

but if they all go one way,
that's the way the wind goes.

William Stafford

ON WEARING EARS

As long as people
continue to wear
ears
there won't
be much
peace and quiet
in this world.

William J. Harris

make it new
  make it new!
cried the parrot
  to the mockingbird...

Lawrence Ferlinghetti

JUST NOW

the grasshopper
that leapt into the
snow-on-the-mountain
chased the white
moth out

David Kherdian

crickets
crickets
crickets
crickets
crickets
crickets
crickets
crickets
crickets
crickets
crickets
crickets
crickets
crickets
crickets
crickets
crickets
crickets
crickets
crickets
crickets
crickets
crickets
crickets
crickets
crickets
crickets

Aram Saroyan

ONCE UPON A TREE

...Once upon a tree
I came across a time,
It wasn't even as
A ghoulie in a dream.

There was a mooly man
Who had a rubber hat
And funnier than that—
He kept it in a can. . . .

Theodore Roethke

AN HISTORIC MOMENT

The man said,
after inventing poetry,
"WOW!"
and did a full somersault.

William J. Harris

The End